Her

Vol. 2

Other books by
Pierre Alex Jeanty

"Her"

"To the Women I Once Loved"

"Unspoken Feelings of a Gentleman"

"Unspoken Feelings of a Gentleman II"

<u>*Coming soon*</u>

"Him"

"HEart"

Her

Vol. II

Pierre Alex Jeanty

jeanius PUBLISHING

Cover Design: Omar Rodriguez
Editor: Carla DuPont Huger
Illustration: TreManda Pewett

ISBN 13: 978-0-9974265-6-4

Jeanius Publishing LLC
430 Lee Blvd
Lehigh Acres, FL 33936

For more information, please visit:
Pierrealexjeanty.com
Jeaniuspublishing.com

Schools & Businesses

Jeanius Publishing books are available at quantity
discounts
with bulk purchases.
For more information please email
contact@jeaniuspublishing.com

To the reader,

Read this more than once,
let the thoughts marinate
savor the depth of these appetizers
suck on the bones of every word.
Digest this body of work.
I made this for you,
I created this for her,
I birthed this for him,
who compares *her* to oxygen.

Enjoy!

To the previous readers,

You've picked up the words that drip from my
heart
and treasured them.
I cannot thank you enough
for supporting what I am doing.
Without you, I'd still exist;
but the poet in me would not have had a voice
loud enough.

Thank you from my heart.

I still do not claim
to be a great poet,
but a great observer of her.

Love will leave few bruises
on several occasions.
It will hit some veins,
and do some damage in parts of you
that the eyes can't see.

But,
it will not give you bullet wounds,
nor will cut deep to the soul
It will never become a bystander while
your heart bleeds to death.

Your voice shouldn't tremble in the midst

of someone who says they love you.

If you are stumbling over your words,

may it be because joy has your knees weak.

But it should never be because of the fact

that fear is swimming through your veins

and doubt overfilling your heart in their presence.

I can't agree with you or them

and say it's love dear.

Falling in love can be scary,

but being in love should never be terrifying.

It was your lack of effort
that screamed, "Let go!"
and whispered, "Move on," to her ears.

Not her friends,
family, or
a possible replacement.

Those who disappear out of your life

as the sun sleeps

are neither lovers or friends.

They are gentle monsters.

They are leeches who will feast until you're

drained.

They are people with terrible promises and rotten

motives.

Do not make them your savior,

do not find comfort on their shoulders,

do not build on their promises.

The caution tapes around her heart
are not there to keep you out,
neither do they exist to be decoration on
Halloween nights.

They are proof of broken entries
by men who hid their true identity
to commit loveless acts.

They are there because
she is guilty of murder against herself,
and them guilty of
being instigators and accomplices.

They are billboards for eyes to see
that she has slept through the worst of
nightmares.

She will remember the moments
you made her feel loved
more than the times you said,
"I love you."

Young love is beautiful,
fall for that boy,
believe that it'll never end,
talk about forever without a care in the world.

However,
do not let old age catch you
doing those things.
It will remind you very quickly,
that boys lie and that a man is what you need.
It will tell you over and over that relationships end
and that in a marriage full of love,
is when you'll being seeing forever.

Young love is beautiful, but old love is real.

Nothing ordinary is meant for you.
There's nothing more unfair to you
than convincing yourself that it is okay
to accept anything short of extraordinary.

Your body is made to be made loved to
by a man who has your 50th wedding anniversary
date marked on his calendar,
leaves his heart in your palms,
and understands the meaning behind a wedding
ring.
Maybe you don't believe in fairy tales,
but "till death tear us apart"
ought to be the least you settle for.

You deserve a love that knows no conditions
and ends at your funeral.

How is it you sacrifice
your happiness
to make sure
there's not a scratch on theirs?

Love should never be
only about your happiness,
neither should it be excluded.

If I must be honest with you,
everyone is forgettable;
though memories may linger and replay
themselves.
It is who we are that makes us unforgettable,
not our want to never be forgotten.
It is the type of love we offer to those who
have never known love that makes us
unforgettable.

Therefore, love hard, despite how hard it is.
It's what they'll remember.

Simple Reminder I

Do not become less of a woman

to a man who is looking for

a woman who thinks less of herself.

Showing less can be seen as more,

but showing them less of who you are

never gets you more.

The scale should never be given
the power to weigh you down.

The number it reads should never
add more burden to your soul.

Beauty is not defined
by how much flesh
rests on your bones,
but how much
compassion is buried in your heart.

If you find those who make you feel ugly
because you weigh more than the average,
tell them to swallow their opinions
and do more than cardio for that ugly heart.

Quit lying through your teeth.
Do not give her a crown
simply because you want her
to bite her tongue.

There's no greater transgression
than attempting to make her feel
that she has fallen short by loving
the way she does.
It is silly to try to convince her
that she is a sinner for being able to love so
devotedly.
It may not be normal to you,
but let it be to her.

***You have to be
more afraid of losing her,***
*than you are afraid
of loving her.*

You will always have those
who will applaud you,
those who will only cheer you on
when life is putting a beating on you.

There will always be those who
want to be in your life,
and those who will stick around
just to be there when things go wrong
so they can have something to
keep them blind to their own misery.

The mistake of many
is that they think *forever*
is a path, rather than a road,
that must be built brick by brick.

Rainbow

How can those who are color blind
see how beautiful a rainbow is?

Those who live in the gray areas
only flirt with the light,
they do not ask its hand in marriage.
You're a rainbow my love,
their sky is too clouded with darkness
for them to see your colors.
You must never let their true color
cause you to lose yours.

You remind me of the bible.

Though people can see between your lines,

they misinterpret your words,

they try to define you by their misunderstanding.

They preach their rumors as truth,

crucify your name,

mock you for being a misfit,

throw dirt on your good intentions,

and bury your character.

Still you rise,

still you overcome,

still you love.

She is tired of empty *I love you's*,
especially the type that trail before "*but*"
to put to sleep the doubts that
whisper reasons to walk away loudly in her ears.

She is sick of promise after promise
made about keeping promises that keep
disappointment tightly hugging her feet.

She isn't bitter, she is sick and tired.
How long do we expect someone to believe
the "nothings" spoken by someone
who is "their everything"?

You can be the type of girl
who boys look at and want more.
But never become the type of woman
who mistakes the hunger in a boy's eyes
for the passion in a man's.

In her smile lives the light
and the darkness of the night sky.
She is no fallen angel,
but an angel who has fallen from grace
quite a few times.
Her prayer is that she finds a man to cheer her
as she puts her halo back the way it belongs.

When their actions

become a brush that meticulously,

stroke by stroke,

reveals the full painting of who they are,

you must not let denial erase

nor paint over their true colors.

They'll be proud of you when you
set your feet in enough success.
Right now, their eyes cannot open
to your dreams.
Fear has stolen their hope
and pocketed their interest for a life that revolves
around things they are passionate about.

Forgive them,
some of them mean well,
some of them don't want their
fear of failing to abuse you
like the fear of failure assaults their minds.

If we love with our lips,

but not our hearts,

we are liars with good intentions,

thieves with charitable actions,

lovers without substance.

Despite,

love is still worth it.

The only love that is worth dying for

is the type of love that makes you feel alive.

Simple Reminder *II*

Wanting someone

who doesn't make you feel wanted,

is wanting everything you don't need.

Needing someone who doesn't live

as if they need you in their life,

is being in need of what you

shouldn't even want.

Do not let the world
turn the sweetness of your smile
into sour tones that hang out
 with ugly words.

Do not give the bad you've seen
the power to plant darkness
in the soil of your soul.

Do not let that ugly past hold the beauty
that lives in your future, hostage.

To the girl looking for love

You are not
a drunk man's playground
just because he has strong arms
and a six pack.
Sober love will always lead to more
memorable moments than drunken lust.

If you do not feed her mind,
your tongue must never find
a way to complain about
the malnourished love
between the two of you.
Nor should it ever question
why her heart has only known
starvation with you.

Beautiful flowers can't bloom
without healthy roots.

Love is a full puzzle;

the bigger picture can

only be seen as you continue

putting the pieces together

and falling deeper and deeper in love.

You will see "*forever*" clearly.

Love is hard to find, but obvious to see.

Her face,

Her laugh,

Her personality

Her existence can make

an atheist

swear that angels exist.

You do so much
to save those dates,
yet never get another day
on their calendar.

By now,
I am praying you see that
it's not who you try to be
tonight for that man
that will make him desire you,
but how true you are to yourself
and what he sees in you.

If you're a size
too big for him to love,
his heart is too many sizes
too small
for him to be your type.

How ignorant
can anyone be
to believe that beauty is
what one looks like,
rather than what can be seen
in one's heart?

Stay in the "now"

If you let the ghost of your past
scare the life
out of your new relationship,
it will haunt you.

You are *made* of love,
How can you let anyone
convince you
that you are not worthy of it?

Self-love
and selfishness
are neither siblings,
neighbors,
or friends.

When you cannot effortlessly
distinguish the difference
between the two,
you've turned self-love into
a self-centered prison.

Don't let any crumbs of attention

he throws at your feet cause you

to bow down to his curse again.

I know you are hungry for love,

but he has proven time

and time again that

he cannot bring enough

to the table to feed you.

Girls like you
give writers like me
things to write about.
You are the blood of my pen,
life to my words.

You are more than art.
You are heaven manifested,
and the sweet imagination
of an innocent soul.
To describe you in shorter words,
is to say that
you are creativity itself to man
and poetry written by God himself.

Simple Reminder *III*

You must be, "Yours,"

before you are anyone else's.

If you wonder
how she carries her baggage so well,
you must first ask her
for a glance at her back.
She has handled betrayal
as if its fire was nothing
more than an illusion.

Women like that handle their flaws,
tame their fears,
and silence their doubts.
Strong doesn't describe her,
she defines strong.

She is the reason men like me
understand what balance is.

When I stare at her, I see both
perfection and imperfection.
I see beauty and ugliness
living in the same place.
I see light and darkness
wrestling one another.

She is so good, yet bad;
a perfect mix of heaven,
with a little hell at times.

She is yours to keep,
but not yours to own.
Yours to lead,
but not yours to lord over.

If we become like those
who failed to love us how
we were meant to be loved,
and treat others the same way
they treated us,
we've become enemies of love
and allies with misery.

Your body must be home to you.

You must find comfort in it.

If you must know, that welcoming smile

is the doorway to the beautiful sky.

That soft voice is honey to the ears of birds.

That heart is oxygen to this earth.

You must risk your heart

to catch love.

This world is all

give and take.

The joy of takers

do not last long.

They tend to

always run out of

things to give

before the givers.

Your curves lead to the ocean,

only those with good driving skills

can handle them.

To many, it won't be the safest route,

they'll miss the turns,

they'll be afraid of being mocked,

they won't be comfortable during the ride.

But love, that's their problem.

Your curves are beautiful.

If they can't love you,

losing more of you shouldn't be the solution.

You are not a fool

*for being **fooled***

***by a fool**.*

Being thick skinned
will do you more good
than being thick.

Out of the men you attract,
some will try to handle you,
but there'll be one who will
help you handle life.

The kind of thickness
you're serving often
determines
who dines at your table.

Get thick sweetheart,
but get that skin thicker
and that heart purer.
They'll walk you further
in this life
than thick thighs ever will.

How can you blame her for choosing herself first
when choosing yourself is your favorite sport?
Women like her have been victims to enough
players, and lost in far too many games.

How can her playing it safe and
being her own MVP be an issue?
The motto that stood as a tagline to your ego used
to be, *"Don't hate the player, hate the game,"* but
now you complain, mouthing off about the game
being unfair and her playing too much.

You can't win them all.

Falling for bad promises is easy.
Our cravings for truthful actions
from someone we love will oftentimes
convince us to see things as they are not.
We become blind and deaf to the truth,
while playing guessing games with the lies,
trying to find which one they'll ever fulfill.

Therefore, forgive yourself.
More than enough of us have been there.

If his actions don't speak
any love languages,
his voice must become
a foreign noise to you.
Reassurance,
quality time,
affection,
and serving you
ought to be found
in what he does
more than what he speaks.

The eyes may lie on some occasions,

but not as often as the ears

do to the heart.

Drugs are liars
who claim they can give
better realities than the current one.

Stupid liars.
They will only silence the hurt
while they feed the pain.

They will promise you freedom
as long you are a slave to them.

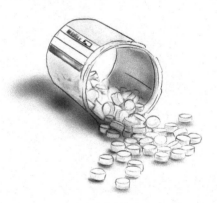

Them not having an appetite for you
does not make you less desirable.

I asked the sky,

"Of all the creations you look down upon,

which would you say is the most beautiful?"

He said, *"Her."*

I smiled knowing that he is as observant as I am.

Simple reminder IV

It is better

     to be soul food

         than to be an

             eye candy,

                 sweetheart.

You may pique her interest,
but you must keep her attention.

You may be granted a date,
but you must court her beyond the courtsides.

You may gain exclusivity,
but you must contribute to her
or gift her presence with your absence.

Have your own,
but do not let it own you.

Be strong, but realize that
loving a man
who is in love with you
does not spell weakness.

Be independent,
but never let yourself
become a man-hater.

Do not give resentment that type of power.

It is not *"men"*
who are your enemy,

but
liars,
manipulators,
and cheaters.

Those exist both
in men and women.

They can't break you.

They don't have the power

to break fighters.

You can only scar warriors;

conquerors are meant to overcome.

You must find the freedom to freely admit
that his touches are still uncomfortable to you
because you've had people who look like him
touch you the same places.

Although without a shadow of a doubt,
you know he is not the same,
he awakes a similar feeling.
Old memories are dug up,
giving breath to skeletons
you hid far beyond your closet.

Listen,
many of us who have seen darkness
don't know how to accept love,
even when our lover accepts our past.

Be honest with him,
tell him you don't know how to love yet,
even when it's everything you want.

Protect your heart,

but don't protect your ego in the process.

It'll cage your heart,

instead of building boundaries around it.

You only kill you
when you live for them.

You kill your dreams,
when you try to convince
your eyes to be one with their vision.

Falling in love
is like going sky diving.
It is exciting,
scary,
and fulfilling.

There will be days
you hit the ground with love,
but you have to get up
to fall further in.

You must be patient
or you'll never be introduced to
the beautiful soul
that is under her mountain
of bad experiences.

Gold isn't found easily.

If love isn't what

you are trying to harvest,

do her a favor and let her know,

so she can make sure

she does not find ground in you

to plan her seed of love.

Recipe for his growth

I am convinced that a man
cannot be a *man*
to a woman, until
he understands
that she is not made
only to feed the appetite
of his lust,
but to nourish his core's
hunger for love.

Gamble with love,

but do not gamble

your heart away to jokers.

Simple reminder V

Give yourself more credit.

Being so stubborn to failure

and so attached to perseverance

is more admirable than

you've led yourself to believe.

You're winning,

even when there aren't enough people cheering.

You cannot love a woman like that
with just words and basic actions.
Do the unusual things that prove
that you're crazy for her.

I cannot tell you what those things
ought to be, but I can tell you that
going to the extreme for real love
doesn't crown you a fool,
but a romantic.

Pierre Alex Jeanty

Her skin is honey

Her heart is gold

Her speech is harmonious

Her love is heavenly

She's been a student of pain,
been in the class of drama,
and circumstances have
yelled at her most of her life.

She wants peace now,
she doesn't want to cradle her problems
in her mind before she sleeps.

She wants to hear less of the world
and do more in her world.

She wants to silence her mind
and listen to God.

If you do not come to contribute to that,
you're a disturbance not a lover.

Your body isn't a hotel room
for men to spend the night
and check out before the sun stands
over the earth.

It was created to be a home
for planting love
and growing a family.

I am a man,
I cannot tell you
what burden she carries,
but I can tell that they are too
heavy for one person to carry.

Nights like this,
she thinks of herself,
what she loves,
what she missed while missing you.

She thinks about what you both were
and could've been.
Then she dreams about what she is going to be.

You are no longer her happiness,
she is what now makes her smile.

Whether you play your hand right or not,

a king will find his way to you.

As long as you hand God your cards to deal.

Love's influence

Her love is powerful.
I am saying this as a man
who has abandoned
many versions of myself
to be better for women like her.

Love is meant to continually blossom.

If it withers overtime,

It is because the soil was not right

Maybe the heart wasn't ready enough,

Or you two were wrong for one another.

I'd bet on the latter.

You not recognizing that you're precious
and that every inch of you
is beautiful,
is your blindness.

Them not recognizing
your worth
and cherishing you,
is their blindness.

The blind cannot lead the blind.
They only find better routes
to mislead each other.

To one man you are not enough;
yet, to another you're more than enough.

If that tells you anything sweetheart,
it's that your worth shouldn't be found in
or determined by a man.

Study her silence,

search her mind

when she is saying nothing.

Her scars should tell you that
she is very capable of healing
and there's a survivor beyond that smile.

You also have to understand that
anyone who has been cut before
is a little afraid of knives,
and every survivor lives with precaution.

Therefore,
she will have fears when it comes to love
and she will be hesitant when it comes to trusting.

Befriend patience.

Simple reminder VI

You're a great catch

that has fallen

into the wrong arms.

If we love with restrictions
and tie it to conditions,
we do not give love room to be love.

When we let true love end,
we experience death.

When we let unpromising love die,
we only begin to live.

Food for thought

You don't need to
sleep with her to know that
she is the woman of your dreams.

What you have to realize
is that she remembers when it ended,
it ended long before she left.

She held on until her hand grew numb,
until she grew too weak to hold on any longer.

She had to convince herself far too many times
to fight for practically nothing.

The memories of how it started
still have a special place in her mind,
but you must know this:

**Her leaving took wrestling against
every part of herself.
Her leaving you is an act of love,
realizing that she has to love herself more
than she cares for you.**

Rake your hands through her hair,

Whisper beautiful words in her ears,

Cup your hands around her beautiful face,

Admire her breath-taking beauty,

Kiss her lips as if they're both

a forbidden fruit

and the sweetest peach you ever tasted.

Hang on to every word that finds its way

out of her mouth.

Let them make a home to your ears,

help them find a space to reside in your memory.

She has had enough with men who heard her,

but did not listen,

nor gave her existence the attention it deserved.

Pierre Alex Jeanty

She is a keeper,
as long as you act like you need her
and treat her like you want to keep her.

Her beauty is timeless.
It is one of those things
that time only betters.

Her skin may inherit wrinkles,
but she will have only left behind
undesirable parts of her by then,
parts of her she needed to outgrow.

Her beauty is timeless,
Perhaps not to the naked eye,
but to those who can see the soul
and listen to the heart.
She only blooms to different stages of beauty.

We risk too much

for the wrong people

and too little

for the right ones.

It's not lost love that we mourn,
but memories.

Love cannot be mourned
as long as both lovers are breathing.

It's the time lost,
the de-attachment,
the moments engraved in the mind,
the death of the feeling that once lived
when things had begun.

As you wait for that moment
when you grow tired enough to walk away,
your legs are also growing tired,
your knees are growing weak in a way they
shouldn't.

Eventually, you won't have enough strength to
walk away as fast as you were supposed to.

Discern

Loyalty is an activist
who fights to
earn your lover's trust,
and the freedom for their heart
to become yours.

However,
it can also be a dictator
your partner uses to keep
your heart imprisoned.

She doesn't want a man
who can fall in love with her,
there's not a doubt that she is lovable.

She needed a man
who would *be* in love with her,
that has been a challenge
many men she has met have faced.

I stared at her
not to search deeper
for flaws,
but because I am amazed by her.

Never in a million years
did I think
love would be wearing
such a gorgeous flesh.

Simple reminder VII

He can't love you

if he has never seen love

in the mirror.

The beauty of surviving and learning

Her lips are made to be kissed by someone
who doesn't condemn the bittersweet flavor
on her tongue.

Someone who can recognize that bitterness
is trying to find roots in her mind,
and see that she isn't settling for that.

Someone who understands that
she has been served the coldest hell,
but is trying to drown her past experiences
and find the courage to embrace new ones.

Her lips are made to be kissed by someone who
can see that she craves the sweetness of life.

Healing happens when you
stop wrestling with the idea that
you gave them power to pin you down
and realize that you simply
got in the ring to fight with good intentions.

You may have lost, but you won yourself back.

If your ego won't let you
compromise for the relationship,
what makes you think
her knowing her self-worth
will let her compromise?

Give no room for her past to whisper lies to you
or to mock her for making mistakes
if you do not want anyone to judge you for yours.

How can you hold on to her past sins
when you only talk about your future as a saint?

She is poetry,
full of emotions
and feelings;
yet complex.
Detailed,
yet unexplainable;
Understood,
yet complicated.

There are hints in the songs she loves,
they may make your ears bleed;
but, they will help you interpret the words
buried under her tongue
and the caged thoughts of her mind.

You are only hard to love
to those who will find walking away easy.

You will be far too much for those
who cannot cherish the idea
of being deeply in love with you.

I think of her as a best seller,
handwritten by God
on pages made from his magnificent robe.

Her choices are every word.
Her eyes are every page.
Her heart is an untold story.

Each chapter may have missing paragraphs,
but the further you get inside
the more she will become easily comprehended.

I advise that you take your time with her;
learning of her has to be a marathon
or you'll sprint past some important details.

A man's hands are made
to cup your face
and his arms to hold you.

The day they become weapons
to terrorize you,
please know that love no longer
lives in that man's heart.

Only anger reigns there.
Anger and love cannot grow in the same garden.

Wait for the man
who makes you question what love is,
one who loves you hard
despite how hard you believe you are to love.

You don't need closure to find happiness again,
you need to find reasons to start a new chapter,
and put down that old book.

Here is one reason, *you deserve to be happy*.

There will

be memories

that live

as long as

you are alive.

Dear,

Giving yourself away
for a cheaper price isn't
the right bait to reel in their love.

Lowering your standard isn't how
you'll get a leg up on anything.

Only *real* love can afford you,
because you are both love and priceless.

Love cannot be a magic trick.
You loving them will not make them right
or make them love you.
The only magic of love is that it can be invisible,
yet seen wherever it exists.

People like her

can only be loved one way.

The right way,

The passionate way,

The self-less way,

One way, different lanes.

Love's agenda is to add to you.

If your love is taking too much from you,

it must be subtracted out of your life.

She doesn't care

whether you are different or not.

What she cares about is

if you're good and right for her.

You may be nothing like the others,

yet still hurt her

when you walk away.

If there's anything more beautiful
than a classy woman with a loving heart,
my eyes have yet to see it.

Simple reminder *VIII*

You don't have to be a model,

it's okay to simply be a woman.

All natural,

all imperfections,

all real.

Every love
starts with forever planted in its yard.
The ones who see it grow,
cultivate their love.

You have to stop
letting his lying tongue
leave marks on your neck
and his hands
leave fingerprints on your back.

Pierre Alex Jeanty

Love was never meant
to be a sword.

Matter of fact, it never is
and never was.

It is the vessels who claim to love us
who put swords to our chests.

A new relationship is not
remedy for heartbreak,
it is rather poison we drink
as we mourn our lovers.

It never gets better,
we simply become worse
with someone else.

The storm will wash away
the façade that those who
aren't true friends put forth.

Prepare for the rain.

How unfortunate

that people with good hearts

sometimes run into bad lovers.

What is more unfortunate

is that many bad lovers are born

from such experiences.

What she doesn't ask for
is usually what she deserves,
the small surprises,
heartwarming gifts,
undivided attention,
and to be showered with compliments.

Never stop trying to impress her.

Being drunk in love
is actually sobering.

It is taking
too many shots of lust
to numb the void
we feel that trips us.
It causes us to land
on the swords aimed for our hearts
that leave scars on our backs.

Love should never be a burden,
even on the hardest days.

She's a skeptic when
it comes to promises.
As she evolves,
she only searches for a love
that can be seen by those who are deaf
and felt by the blind.

Do not ask for her heart

if you cannot give her your time.

A lot of wrong men
will fight for you;
how you pick the right one
is by keeping your eyes on
which of them doesn't know
how to stop fighting.

You are not wrong for demanding
that he puts boundaries around
the happy home you are trying to build.

He calls it insecurity, but you see it as
keeping away the women who treat
men as pets and are looking to kidnap a new one.

Enough female dogs have wandered
into nice neighborhoods, snuck through open
doors and sabotaged nice homes.

Sweetheart, you have every right to want
the door of your relationship closed and secured.

Affection ought to be part
of your routine rather than
something you treat her to
once in a blue moon.
Imagine if the earth saw
the moon every so often.

Simple reminder IX

Beauty

is in the eye

of the beholder.

Behold

what you see in that mirror.

She is a cup of good,
stirred with bad,
and a few drops of innocence.
With a crooked smile,
and an adventurous laugh.

Naïve, she is at times.
But behind all those things,
is hidden a girl
who doesn't always take a mature path.
Bad intentions leak out of her at times,
but she is far from evil.

I am not saying this to condemn her,
but to remind you,
that even the prettiest people
have some ugliness planted in them.

It's the reality of life.

New love cannot find its way into the lives of those who are held captive by yesterday.

She is a heavenly being
trapped in this dark world.
There is nothing I'd like to do more
than remind her
to never let the darkness oppress her
and lead her to forget
that she is made of light.

You cannot love and doubt simultaneously.

If the doubt is more alive,

it is because it is being fed well.

Eventually, it will eat away the love

that was ever on the table, piece by piece.

When love is fed,

you will vomit almost every ounce of doubt.

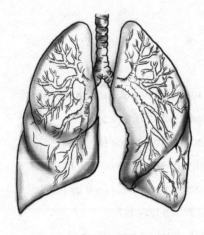

Boldness flowed through her veins
and grace filled her lungs.
Women like her know when
to raise their voice
and when to let their silence
make the noise.

You're the sun sweetheart,

even on the cloudy days,

you are made to shine.

At this point in her life,
she isn't looking for a man
to tell her she is pretty,
she's dying to meet the one
who will run out of words,
trying to explain
why she is beautiful to him.

If you pay enough attention,
you will realize that there is something beautiful
about making her feel beautiful.

Real recognize real

There are many women who hide
behind a fake boldness.
They try to bury their desire
for the love of a man,
into their independence.

But you, you understand
what it means to be
your own and someone else's.
You love yourself
in a pure and honest way,
and that is what good men are searching for.

Enough men wait until
it all ends to love their woman
like they did when it all started.

You shouldn't take such chances with her.

She'll fight a war for love,
but she will never fight for
your time nor attention.

Being normal is over praised.
You were never meant
to be accepted by all.
Therefore, be as weird
and as odd as you want to be.

True love is without
conditions and boundaries,
nor is it at the mercy of reciprocity;
however, love must be reciprocated
in order to mature.

I'd like to take this moment
to celebrate you.

To heal after having your heart broken
countless times is an accomplishment.

Many don't graduate past the pain.
They only pick up a third degree burn on their
soul while bitterness and anger become their first
and second degrees respectively.

Message from the guy who loves you

Allow me to hold your hands,
Allow my fingers to tightly hug yours,
Allow yourself to be naked while being fully
dressed around me,
Allow those guards to rest,
Allow yourself to be at ease, to entertain the idea
of being loved in a way your defensive ways won't
let you.
Allow the doors of your heart to open up a little bit
and let some fresh air in,
Allow me to see the real you, the vulnerable you.
I am not asking for you to fall in love with me yet,
but please be yourself around me.
That is all I'm asking.

Love's words

I am nothing

to be afraid of.

When you meet me,

you will see.

Women like her are rare
not because of what they look like,
nor what they have,
but it is because of who they are
and how they view this thing called life
despite the troubles it lays at their feet.

Dear Alexa,

I cannot wait to meet you.
I will be obsessed with you, I already am now.

Side note: *Your name begins and ends with the first letter of the alphabet. If I ever fail to put you first, remember that's the position you deserve and ought to settle for when a man asks for your heart.*

Simple reminder X

Treat her as if

she is both

gold and glass.

Thank You

About the Author

Pierre Alex Jeanty, Founder of Gentlemenhood™ and CEO of Jeanius Publishing, is a Haitian-American author, poet, and influencer, who is devoted to making an impact through his writing. He primarily focuses on poetically sharing his journey, lessons, and mistakes along the paths of manhood and love. Pierre vows to share his wisdom with all, in hopes of inspiring men to become better, and to be a voice of hope to women who have lost faith in good men. This is the vision of his brand, and the agenda he follows as a writer.

Pierre currently resides in southwest Florida with his family and travels as a speaker as he continues to write.

You can contact him through pierrealexjeanty.com
And find him on
Instagram: PierreJeanty
Facebook: Pierre Alex Jeanty
Twitter: PierreAJeanty
and other social networks by searching his name.